Lift Up
Your Heart

Poetic Reflections for the Seasons of Faith

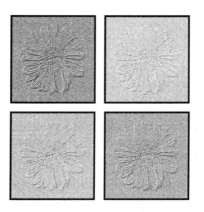

Rev. Msgr. Gerald J. Walsh

Scripture passages quoted in this book are from the *New American Catholic Bible*, copyright ©1971, Catholic Book Publishing Company, New York, New York.

Other titles by Msgr. Gerald J. Walsh available at E. T. NEDDER Publishing include *God Still Calls, Vocation Stories of Real Seminarians.*

For further information visit our website at www.nedderpublishing.com or contact the publisher at the address listed below.

Additional copies of this publication may be acquired by sending check or money order for $10.95 plus $4.00 postage and handling to: E. T. NEDDER Publishing, PMB #299, 9121 East Tanque Verde, Suite 105, Tucson Arizona 85749-8390. Or call toll free 1-877-817-2742. Fax: 1-520-760-5883.

ISBN 1-893757-22-6

10 9 8 7 6 5 4 3 2

TABLE OF CONTENTS

III. ORDINARY SEASONS OF THE YEAR

FOREWORD

Poetry, they say, is the language of the heart. I truly believe this is true, since I have found it so. Poetry is also a mystery to me. It comes and goes like gentle breezes and if you catch a line and go with it, amazing things can happen. I must admit that I do not understand poetry. And, like all things which I do not understand, I stand in awe of how the words and concepts come together to make imminent sense.

At other times, one must take time to "reflect" upon the words to discover new and exciting meanings hidden within them. This reflection often allows individual interpretations to flourish so that no one person may ever say that he or she has the "real sense" of the verse, excluding all others. That is the beauty of poetry and the joy of those who read, relish, enjoy, reflect upon and discover what no one else may ever see

The verses contained in this book are not meant to be profound in meaning. Rather, they are simple reflections on life. Some of them are based on Scriptural stories. Others are impressions expressing reactions to the presence of God in nature and the world around us. Some of them are written in free verse while others are arranged in rhyme. They are intended to be easy reading, easily understandable and gentle on one's mind.

It might be well for me to tell you that my first poetic inspiration began many years ago when I was a student in the seminary. Occasionally I would pen verses for our school publication. After leaving the seminary and beginning my busy priestly ministry there was little time for verses. It has only been during this past year of retirement that I have been led to return to putting poetic lines together to express the enchantment of my life.

The number of poetic reflections in this book is 72 - a very biblical number - one chosen, not by accident but by design. In St. Luke's Gospel, Chapter 10, we read that Jesus "appointed a further 72 and sent them in pairs before him to every town and place he intended to visit."

In that sense, I hope that these "72" poetic reflections will "go out" from these pages to inspire, encourage, impress and touch many lives, and bring some comfort to you, the kind and gentle reader, so that these poetic rhymes may truly be the language which speaks to and "lifts up your heart" in joy.

–Gerald J. Walsh

ACKNOWLEDGMENTS

I am very grateful to my dear friends, Dick and Ellie Steehler of Tucson, Arizona, for their encouragement and support. Their faith in me and their love of poetry has been a very great factor in the writing of this book. There were times when I would have given up the project had it not been for their interest and help.

My gratitude to Father Kenneth Phillips whose computer expertise has been a gift to me in the work of putting the written word together in proper sequence and form.

Special thanks to Marge Grosz, my friend and mentor, who spent long hours editing and preparing the copy for the printer.

May God be with each of you and send you his blessings.

DEDICATION

In memory of my dear sisters,
Lucille Janet and Lois Marie,
who are with God.
May the beauty and poetry
of their lives,
which has touched all of us
who knew and loved them,
remind us to "lift up our hearts" often
in joy and praise of our God.

PART I.

Seasons of Advent and Christmas

"In the sixth month, the angel Gabriel was sent from God to a town of Galilee named Nazareth, to a virgin betrothed to a man named Joseph, of the house of David. The virgin's name was Mary." Luke 1:26-27

Nazareth

Come quickly, Gabriel.
The virgin maiden,
quietly in Nazareth
awaits, unknowingly,
the messenger of God.

How can this be?
She hesitates
and all creation
holds its breath.

Isaiah and all the prophets,
who foretold through prophecy;
Adam and Eve
and all of their children
grow impatient.

It is so long to have waited.
King David,
and all of the kings,
watch for the
King of Kings.

Please, Mary, you
have found favor
with God.

Please, Virgin Maiden,
have no fear -
The Holy Spirit will come.

Please Mary, long have we
waited for redemption,
for open gates,
for a glimpse of our God.

Please Mary,
now is the time.
We are ready, and
the world is hushed in
anticipation...PLEASE !

"I am the handmaid
of the Lord,
let it be done to me
according to your word.
Thank you, Mary!
All creation,
heaven and earth,
EXULTS
for God has come!

"All this happened to fulfill what the Lord had said through the prophet:
 'The Virgin shall be with child
 and give birth to a son,
and they shall call him Emmanuel.'"
    Matthew 1:22-23

Advent

Quickly comes the purpled season
calling us to other times.
And it gives us every reason
to release the tie that binds.

Binds us to this lowly world
of such fleeting life below.
While a heaven waits, unfurled,
rich with promise to bestow.

To bestow to every soul
whose fragile future isn't clear.
Seeking now to be consoled
and released from every fear.

Fear which often comes between us
when we dwell upon our sins.
Only love can lift and cleanse us
like the "Dew Dropped Down" by him.

Bethlehem is where we hasten;
children watching for his birth.
In our hearts and souls, now chastened
for his coming new on earth.

"And behold, Elizabeth, your relative, has also conceived a son in her old age, and this is the sixth month for her who was called barren; for nothing will be impossible for God." Luke 1:36

Elizabeth

Elizabeth,
ancient cousin,
bent by burdening years,
suddenly is fertile, fallow ground
for new life.

Zachary knows, and yet,
does not know how!
Mystery!
Years of fervent prayer,
 bordering despair,
 why now fulfilled
 in twilight years?

Monstrous, heavy shame
on aged shoulders stooped,
now lifted.
At long last, head high, eyes brimming,
vindication by news of prodigy.

Toil worn hands,
and speech loosed tongue,
lift
in Benediction
to God - the giver!
"His name is John!"

"And so Joseph went from the town of Nazareth in Galilee to Judea, to David's town of Bethlehem-- because he was of the house and lineage of David--to register with Mary, his espoused wife, who was with child. While they were there the days of her confinement were completed. She gave birth to her first-born son and wrapped him in swaddling clothes and laid him in a manger because there was no room for them in the place where travelers lodged." Luke 2: 4-6

Bethlehem

The urgent longing of our hearts
is voiced in plaintiff tones
as passionately we implore
in grave and painful groans

the coming of our God and King
to hasten, now at last
to come and fill our hearts with love,
and banish darkness past.

Then suddenly, he does appear
in splendor and acclaim.
He bursts into our sinful world,
no power, honor or fame.

But in a humble empty cave
where cattle find their rest,
the Christ, the Savior of the world,
is born from one who's blest.

And every mother's child of us
who seeks salvation's grace,
is richer now that he has come
to save the human race.

"There lived in Jerusalem at the time a certain man named Simeon. He was just and pious, and awaited the consolation of Israel, and the Holy Spirit was upon him. It was revealed to him by the Holy Spirit that he would not experience death until he had seen the Anointed of the Lord. He came to the temple now inspired by the Spirit; and when the parents brought in the child Jesus to perform for him the customary ritual of the law, he took him in his arms and blessed God...." Luke 2:25-28

Simeon

The temple was filled with crowds that day,
as the aged Simeon made his way
across the court to the open door
with painful steps on the dusty floor.

Someone said that "the family" was there,
so, led by the Spirit, he came to stare
with eyes so dim he could hardly see,
and yet he knew that this could be

the One whom his heart had longed to hold
in his arms which often ached to enfold
this Child of destiny, Child of the rise
and fall of many whose searching eyes

looked for the future of Israel
like listening for the sound of a distant bell,
ringing out joyful tones of hope
for a nation still trying to grasp and grope

for peace in the midst of pain and sin,
in a world where joy might enter in,
now that the Savior had truly come
and his own long anxious life had run

its course. As he held this boy he knew
fulfillment, as his patient life now drew
to a happy close as he reverently blessed
the God who finally gave him rest.

"When the day came to purify them according to the law of Moses, the couple brought him up to Jerusalem so that he could be presented to the Lord, for it is written in the law of the Lord, 'Every first-born male shall be consecrated to the Lord.' They came to offer in sacrifice 'a pair of turtle doves or two young pigeons,' in accord with the dictate in- the law of the Lord." Luke 2: 22-24

The Turtle Doves

In mournful tones
the turtle dove calls
as early as each day is born.
It calls for a mate - its other half,
in convincing melody.

Does it remember that fateful day,
O Jerusalem,
two turtle doves were offered?
Such a ransom - total gift of self -
to buy back so noble a first born.

Does the memory linger,
as the dove calls and pleads
for a soul-mate to make a pair
for "him" once again,
echoing down the corridors
of timeless temples?

"Suddenly the angel of the Lord appeared in a dream and said to him, 'Joseph, son of David, have no fear about taking Mary as your wife. It is by the Holy Spirit that she has conceived this child. She is to have a son and you are to name him Jesus because he will save his people from their sins.' All this happened to fulfill what the Lord had said ..." Matthew 1: 20-22

Joseph

You are not the Joseph of many brothers.
You did not have a coat unlike the others.
You were not sold into slavery as a boy.
You are not the son who was Jacob's joy.

Who are you, Joseph, husband of Mary,
chosen by God, blessed and strengthened
    to carry,

to protect, to father the Son of God
　as your own,
knowing at each step that you were not alone?

Silent, prayerful Joseph, full of constant faith,
walking softly through the mysteries,
the dreams that gave,
you courage and hope as you fulfilled
　your call
to provide and protect so no danger
　would befall

the gentle mother and her son, Emmanuel,
whose coming announced that soon all
　　would be well.
But you, like the other Joseph, had dreams too
causing you to question for what reason
　it was you

whom God had need of to foster care his son
　until the day when his mission had begun.
And so to Egypt, like the Joseph of old
you took the child and Mary, as the angel
　had foretold.

Your heart was full of worry, anxious for their
  care,
as you recalled your namesake who also
  had been there,
a stranger among strangers in a land
  so far away
waiting for the summons to send you
  on your way.

O Joseph, patient guardian,
such faith and trust you showed,
before the angels' messages you,
humble servant, bowed,
as slowly you, with obedient heart,
back home did make your way
to Nazareth, your own village,
to live out all your days.

"When John the Baptizer made his appearance as a preacher in the desert of Judea, this was his theme: 'Reform your lives! The reign of God is at hand.' It was of him that the prophet had spoken when he said: 'A herald's voice in the desert;
Prepare the way of the Lord,
make straight his paths.'"   Matthew. 3:1-3

A Voice in the Desert

The cry of the Baptist
is heard in our land:
John, in camel's hair
passionately pleads
with every soul
to repent.

The sound of salvation
as Isaiah speaks,
beckons - invites -
begs and commands us
to prepare his way, and
to long for freedom, and
to repent.

The heart is suddenly clutched
and held in sweet embrace,
as grace lifts and touches,
and moves one eagerly
to repent.

The Eternal God is here,
Emmanuel,
reaching out in love,
ready, waiting and longing
to forgive!
O come!

PART II.

Seasons of
Lent and Easter

"Comfort, give comfort to my people, says your God.
Speak tenderly to Jerusalem,
 and proclaim to her that her service is at an end,
 her guilt is expiated."   Isaiah 40:1-2

Comfort Ye, My People

How swiftly flow the tides of time.
How gently comes the rise and rhyme
of days and nights like links of chain,
appear, are gone, then come again.

The weaving of the grace of God
into our daily human needs,
the presence of a shepherd's care
gives courage as he daily pleads

for all our unimportant tasks,
which seem so absolutely dear,
so necessary for our peace,
and yet, their use is not that clear.

But God, who looks into our hearts,
as we seek him with all our might,
and sees our special worth apart
from all that clutters up our sight,

is patient with our basic faults,
as knowing we are slow to learn,
he waits and waits upon our choice
until at last we homeward turn.

Then swift to welcome and embrace,
and swift to make us feel our best,
he wraps his arms around our hearts
and sings our longing souls to rest.

"While he was still speaking a crowd came, led by the man named Judas, one of the Twelve. He approached Jesus to embrace him. Jesus said to him, 'Judas, would you betray the Son of Man with a kiss?'" Luke 22:47-48

Tragic Night

They came to take him in the dark
    on that disgraceful night.
With swords and clubs they came for him.
He showed no sign of fright.

Would they have done this in the light
    with everyone to see?
It seems that darkness hides our shame
    and gives us bravery.

How tragic that it had to be.
So patiently he went.
The quick betrayal took no time.
The thirty coins were spent.

The time had come for him to be
    a victim for our sin;
and all at once all reason fled
    and Satan entered in.

Just when did Judas see his deed
    as shameful as it was?
How tragic that his life should end
    with such a sense of loss.

The question of his last desire,
    the mental agony
he suffered on that ugly night
    remains a mystery.

If he had watched one hour with him,
    with Peter, James and John.
    would he have done this shameful thing?
Instead, he was quickly gone.

The Father's will for us was sealed.
His son would die in pain.
Our sins were cause for cruel death
   but he would rise again.

The mystery of our redemption, then
   is such a gift for me.
All pieces somehow do make sense
   when comes eternity.

"When noon came, darkness fell on the whole countryside and lasted until midafternoon. At that time Jesus cried in a loud voice, '*Eloi, eloi, lama sabachtani*?' which means, 'My God, my God, why have your forsaken me?'" Mark 15:33-34

In Cruce Salus

In meditation's pensive mood
Two trees were pictured there.
Upon the one a man was hung.
The other tree was bare.

The first was called "The Tree of Life".
The second that of "Death".
The tree of Death had only nails.
The first had Living Breath.

The Tree of Death was offered me.
At once I did accept.
Then dying, I gave up my life.
But Living Breath I kept.

Then with my cross I followed him,
and he encouraged me.
And with his arms outstretched toward mine,
I spent eternity.

"There were also women present looking on from a distance. Among them were Mary Magdalene, Mary the mother of James the younger and Joses, and Salome. These women had followed Jesus when he was in Galilee and attended to his needs...." Mark 15: 40-41

Stabat Mater

A knowing breeze was blowing now.
The awful stillness sounded
   no more in guilty ears.
But realization thundered slowly
   and persecutors vanished -
   their hate betrayed by tears.

A woman bent with agony
   stood sentry-like apart
   from others...seeming alone.
For overhead her son was dead!
From nail-dug wounds suspended
   the "rejected cornerstone."

The sins of men were murderous
   in demanding Life Divine
   as heaven's entry fee.
But a sword pierced heart its "fiat" sung,
   as in hope of resurrection
   she remembered his decree.

"They took Jesus' body and, in accordance with Jewish burial custom, bound it up in wrappings of cloth and perfumed oils. In the place where he had been crucified there was a garden, and in the garden a new tomb in which no one had ever been buried. Because of the Jewish Preparation Day they buried Jesus there, for the tomb was close at hand." John 19:40-42

Pieta

The warm soft touch of a living child
    returns to memory now;
as a cold dark cross surrenders him
    to outstretched arms below.

The stiff still limbs are weighted down
    with the heaviness of death.

For there is no beat in the broken heart,
  and from bleeding lips, no breath.

But peace remains in her grieving heart
  though death seems everywhere;
As mother holds her lifeless son
  and "fiat" is her prayer.

"Thus has Jesus become the guarantee of a better covenant. Under the old covenant there were many priests because they were prevented by death from remaining in office; but Jesus, because he remains forever, has a priesthood which does not pass away. Therefore he is always able to save those who approach God through him, since he forever lives to make intercession for them."   Hebrews 7:22-25

Ex Malo Bonus

After many years of suffering,
suffering from strife and war,
came an era of good fortune,
fortune never seen before.

Like a breeze it swept the country,
country waiting for release,
and it brought unheard of teaching,
teachings based on love and peace.

32

Then the breeze was quickly stifled,
stifled as a child in birth,
but its life to us was given,
given to remain on earth.

Many years have followed after,
after man's ungrateful show,
but the memory still lingers,
lingers and will never go.

For this bringer of good tidings,
tidings brought for our release,
will not leave us without comfort,
comfort and eternal peace.

"They led him away under arrest and brought him to the house of the high priest, while Peter followed at a distance. Later they lighted a fire in the middle of the courtyard and were sitting beside it, and Peter sat among them. A servant girl saw him sitting in the light of the fire. She gazed at him intently, then said, 'This man was with him.' He denied it, saying, 'Woman, I do not know him.' A little while later someone else saw him and said, 'You also are one of them too.' But Peter said, 'No sir, not I...' At the very moment he was saying this, a cock crowed. The Lord turned around and looked at Peter...He went out and wept bitterly." Luke 22:54-62

Bitter Memories

The shameful scene again unfolds,
the drama of my fears.
Again I live through every thought,
my heart is full of tears.

Although my soul is now at peace,
the memory still remains
of my denial of my Lord,
like deep disgraceful pains.

The figure on the pavement there,
could that be Christ my Lord?
The heavy cross has been too much,
much blood has been outpoured.
The weakness of the victim now
is obvious to all.
There, Simon of Cyrene will help,
he feels a special call.

If I just keep my distance now,
no one need ever know.
That servant girl is watching me,
I'll crouch by the fire, low,
as I draw near to warm myself
but wait, she looks again;
"You, too, were one of his," she says
my heart is now in pain.

"I do not even know the man,"
I blurt out with such force
that everyone now looks at me.
The lie now runs its course.
Just then I hear the cock crow.
Three times the warning comes.
And then he's there - and looks at me.
"Oh, God, what have I done?"

My broken heart wells up within
and tears begin to flow.
"How could I do this dreadful deed?"
Repentance seems so slow.

Just then another memory serves -
"Do you love me, Peter?" he said.
Three times I promised that I did
and that his sheep be fed.
So often, since, my aching heart
reminds me of my sin;
and how my sorrow opened it
to let him enter in.

"Early in the morning on the first day of the week, while it was still dark, Mary Magdalene came to the tomb. She saw that the stone had been moved away, so she ran off to Simon Peter and the other disciple (the one Jesus loved) and told them, 'The Lord has been taken from the tomb! We don't know where they have put him!'"   John 20: 1-3

The Holy Sabbath

How empty seemed their lives that day,
unlike the tomb where Jesus lay.
Their hearts were sad and heavy too,
as though, with all their doubts, they knew

that he had said that he would rise
and yet, they could not realize
just what he meant, what he would do,
and so they waited, as they grew

more fearful of the soldiers near,
who also feared that they would bear
his body off to some strange place
and then proclaim that by some grace

he had risen as he said,
and then the news would soon be spread
that he, indeed, was God's own Son.
Then this "New Way" would have begun.

And so such thoughts about the way
sad things had happened just that day,
were everywhere in people's minds,
to cause them wonder and remind

them of his promise, always kept
even when his friends had slept
that fateful hour of his arrest,
which they would know was not their best.

And yet, in this dark hour of pain,
as they sat down to wait again,

his words were clear and yet it all
was so unreal, like some dark pall.

And so, they waited by the tomb
as though it was a waiting room,
so, if it happened, they would see
their Lord again in majesty.

And then a sudden burst of light
and gone was every star of night,
and there he was in glory dressed
and all their fears he then addressed.

"Why look for life among the dead?
For I have risen as I said,
and now you, too, must rise with me
to live new lives of mystery.

For now I go to make a place
where you without a single trace
of sin will follow me someday,
and there, forever, with me will stay."

"He said to them: 'Thus it is written that the Messiah must suffer and rise from the dead on the third day. In his name, penance for the remission of sins is to be preached to all the nations, beginning at Jerusalem. You are witnesses of this. See, I send down upon you the promise of my Father. Remain here in the city until you are clothed with power from on high.'"
Luke 24: 46-49

Alleluia!!

Someone has walked this way before.
There's blood on the gatepost
and blood on the floor
of the place where the ruffians came
to cry shouts of insult
and shout cries of shame.

Someone has fallen on the cold hard street,
fallen like a soldier,
tortured and beat.
Lifeless and deathlike someone fell.
How heavy the burden?
No one can tell.

Someone has hung on a rough hewn cross
between two thieves
who resented their loss.
Someone nailed for the world to see,
someone willing
to die for me.

Someone was placed in an unused tomb,
someone hidden away
in nature's womb.
Then someone rose on Easter Day
to proclaim eternal life
in a great new way.
ALLELUIA !

"It happened that one of the Twelve, Thomas, (the name means 'Twin') was absent when Jesus came. The other disciples kept telling him, 'We have seen the Lord!' His answer was, 'I will never believe it without probing the nail prints in his hands, without putting my finger in the nail marks and my hand into his side.'" John 20:24-25

Doubting Thomas

"Unless I put my finger in the nail prints,
Unless I touch the wound upon his side,
I simply can't believe that he is risen.
I'm sorry that your words must be denied.

It's all too much, too terribly overwhelming.
It's way beyond my faith to think he lives.
The tragic death he died was so consuming.
How can it be that now to us he gives

himself as risen from the empty tomb?
As living once again, no longer dead?
What does it all mean for us, his brothers?
My soul is troubled, filled with fear and
dread."

The others simply sat and slowly listened.
Their own doubts and fears were yet to be
addressed.
As Thomas spoke with such deep down
conviction,
their own emotions hard upon them pressed.

Then suddenly he stood alive among them.
Through doorways locked and barred he
came.
The beauty of his Person overwhelmed them.
So dumbfounded, they could not recall their
name.

He told them then in words, "To be at peace,"
and turning he asked Thomas to touch his
  side
so that he might now believe that he had risen
  and now with them, forever, would abide.

Words of faith and honor then were spoken,
"My Lord and God," was all that Thomas
    could say.
For Christ, his Lord, now truly had arisen,
    and "Doubting Thomas" faith-filled, knelt
    to pray.

"Two of them that same day were making their way to a village named Emmaus seven miles distant from Jerusalem, discussing as they went all that had happened. In the course of their lively exchange, Jesus approached and began to walk along with them. However, they were restrained from recognizing him..." Luke 24:13-16

Emmaus Journey

He came so suddenly that day from nowhere
    so it seemed,
and walked along the road with us, as from
    our hearts their streamed
the sadness of those recent days, recalling
    painful sights.
We could not understand just how he'd
    missed those days and nights.

We thought that all Jerusalem had heard of
    Jesus' death.
The Master who so many thought would bring
    a welcome breath
of freedom to our suffering lives, and give us
    hope once more.
But they had killed him violently and left us
    sad and poor.

Then he began to speak to us of all that had
    taken place,
interpreting the Sacred Word with clarity and
    grace.
When suddenly we found ourselves at a place
    of food and rest;
we begged him to come in with us, our
    burning hearts confessed

a longing to remain with him - a space now
    filled with hope;
and so he sat and broke the bread - our minds
    could scarcely cope

with overwhelming disbelief that he was
   really there.
Then suddenly he disappeared, like shadows
   in the air.

So, quickly then did we retrace our steps to
   tell the news
to all our friends, who now at last, no longer
   could refuse
to trust his words that he had risen and was
   no longer dead;
that we had seen him on the road and knew
   him breaking bread!

"One day he got into a boat with his disciples and said to them, 'Let us cross over to the far side of the lake.' So they set out, and as they sailed, he slept. A windstorm descended on the lake, and they began to ship water and be in danger. They came to awaken him, saying, 'Master, master, we are lost.' He awoke and rebuked the wind and the tumultuous waves. The waves subsided and it grew calm. Then he asked them, 'Where is your faith....?'" Luke 8:22-25

Fragile Folks

So patiently he waits for us
among the crumbs of living.
So little does he ask of us.
So little is our giving.
He lets us make our own mistakes.
He doesn't interfere.
He waits for us to turn to him.
He lingers ever near.

So independent are we all,
in most of life's demands.
So self-sufficient, so we think;
so strong, so proud, so grand.
And then at once the moment comes.
How weak we mortals be.
We fail the test and tumble down
to frail mortality.

We weep and cry for someone's help.
We stretch our hands to him.
We offer to amend our ways.
We promise no more sin.
And then, because he loves us so,
he's anxious to forgive.
So reaching down he lifts us up,
and once again, we live.

"You have visited the land and watered it;
greatly have you enriched it.
God's watercourses are filled;
you have prepared the grain.
Thus have you prepared the land:
drenching its furrows,
breaking up its clods,
Softening it with showers,
blessing its yield."   Psalm 65:10-11

Refreshed

The raindrops sparkle on the lilac bush.
Like pouring gems, they come.
Their beauty casts a glimmering touch
to streams which quickly run.

The earth is washed and cleansed again.
There is freshness everywhere.
God pours his cleansing water down
to show his love and care.

The tears of joy are on my face;
I know his love for me.
"If you were alone upon the earth,
I still would die for thee."

So wash me yet again, My Lord.
Drop down your cleansing dew
to freshen memories once more
and gather us anew.

Part III.

Ordinary Seasons of the Year

"When Jesus came to the neighborhood of Caesarea Philippi, he asked his disciples this question: 'Who do people say that the Son of Man is?' They replied, 'Some say John the Baptist, other Elijah, still others Jeremiah or one of the prophets.' 'And you,' he said to them, 'who do you say that I am?' 'You are the Messiah,' Simon Peter answered, 'the Son of the living God!' Jesus replied, 'Blest are you Simon, son of Jonah! No mere man has revealed this to you, but my heavenly Father. I, for my part declare to you, you are 'Rock,' and on this rock I will build my church, and the jaws of death shall not prevail against it. I will entrust to you the keys of the kingdom of heaven. Whatever you declare bound on earth shall be bound in heaven; whatever you declare loosed on earth shall be loosed in heaven." Matthew 16:13-19

Simon Peter

Simon, Simon, do not fear.
Leave your boat and fishing gear.

Listen to your fishing brother,
then follow me for I've another
task for you and Andrew, too,
for the present time; and then a new
and different life will soon be yours,
away from nets and boats and oars.

And if you love me, as you say,
there soon will come another day
when "Peter" shall become your name
and nothing then will be the same.
For upon your name my church will stand
like "rock" in spite of hell's demands,
whose evil gates shall not prevail.
On other seas, your barque will sail

as "Fisher of Men", you now are cast
as "Vicar" you stand before the mast,
with eleven others who soon will be
apostles who will speak for me.
In spite of cock-crow and denial
you will repent in tears, then I'll

forgive and you will find
the grace to loose and grace to bind

the sins of other as you heal
those suffering souls and make them feel
my presence through your gentle touch,
and they will know how very much

I love them through your constant word,
and I, as Shepherd, I as Lord,
will gather my sheep as ages run
and to my Sheepfold they will come.
For you will feed my lambs, my sheep,
until, at last, you too, will sleep
upon the cross as I have done,
and home to me, then, you will come.

O Simon, Simon, do not fear.
Leave your boat and fishing gear.
Listen to your fishing brother
and follow me for I've another
place for you above the rest
where you will be forever blest.

"As Jesus went, the crowds almost crushed him. A woman with a hemorrhage of twelve years' duration, incurable at any doctor's hands, came up behind him and touched the tassel on his cloak. Immediately, her bleeding stopped. Jesus asked, 'Who touched me?'...'Someone touched me; I know that power has gone forth from me.'... She came forward trembling. .... Daughter, it is your faith that has cured you. Now go in peace.'" Luke 8:42-48

Just One Touch

"If only I can touch his robe,
I will be healed," she said.
"If only he will look at me,
he'll know how much I've bled.

If only for one single second,
he'll look into my eyes.
If only I could speak to him
and make him realize

how much I've suffered every day
for many wretched years.
If only I could touch his heart,
he'd wipe away my tears.

If only I could reach beyond
this crowd, which presses so,
I do believe his strength would come.
I don't believe, I know!

Ah, there, I finally brushed his cloak,
but wait, he's turning round.
"Who touched me?" as he scans the crowd,
searching for one bound

by chains of pain and agony
for years beyond recall,

then eyes are met in sympathy,
and power goes out to all.

But special healing now is felt
by one whose faith is strong;
by one who knew his touch would heal,
and fill her heart with song.

"When Jesus looked up and caught sight of a vast crowd coming toward him, he said to Philip, 'Where shall we buy bread for these people to eat?' (He knew well what he intended to do but he asked this to test Philip's response.) Philip replied, 'Not even with two hundred days' wages could we buy loaves enough to give each of them a mouthful!'… There is a lad here who has five barley loaves and a couple of dried fish, but what good is that for so many?' Jesus said, 'Get the people to recline.' " John 6: 5-9

Loaves and Fishes

The hungry crowd kept pressing on
not knowing what might be.
They only knew that he was there.
They waited now to see

what strange new miracle he might work.
What limb or sense he'd heal.
Each one was hoping for some sign
as they began to feel
a strange and different hunger pain;
a need that he might call
and then from nowhere, so it seemed,
were fish and bread for all.

Among the vast and curious crowd
the young lad's food was shared.
Twelve baskets full of remnants then
were left, as they declared
this truly is the prophet sent
to save the world from sin.
And they were ready then and there
to make him their own king.

How could they miss the point that day?
How could they be so blind?
The hunger that he satisfied
so briefly, should remind

them of his greater gift of food;
himself, the Bread of Life,
which he would give some later day
the night before the strife.

How deeply do we hunger too.
How much we long for him.
In Eucharistic union now,
as food, he enters in
to satisfy our need for grace,
the hunger of our hearts.
Yet not completely are we filled
as long as he's apart
from us in this short life.
And it will always be.
Our hearts are never satisfied
until eternity.

"The mother of Zebedee's sons came up to him accompanied by her sons, to do him homage and ask of him a favor. ...Whoever wants to rank first among you must serve the needs of all."   Matthew 20: 20-27

First Places

James and John, why did your mother
approach and ask for favors new?
Did she not know about the others
who might wish that favor too?

To be the first among all others,
friends who also had been called,
men who really were like brothers,
no surprise they were appalled!

Jesus put it very clearly:
"Can you drink the cup I must?"
and you answered very nearly,
"Yes, with confidence and trust."

Then he said in certain phrases,
first places were not his to give.
Serving others in all phases
is the way we're called to live!

Was your mother disappointed
when she heard the words he spoke?
Words which somehow then anointed
you, so selfish bonds were broke,

and new freedom then was given.
Pride no longer drove your heart,
rather, "Christ like" now you're driven
never to be placed "apart."

"Come to me, all you who are weary and find life burdensome, and I will refresh you. Take my yoke upon your shoulders and learn from me, for I am gentle and humble of heart. Your souls will find rest, for my yoke is easy and my burden light." Matthew 11:28-30

Eucharist

So quietly and patiently the tabernacle rests.
Its Eucharistic occupant eternally alert
and ministering, each moment,
even as we sleep.

Vigilant in night watch or morning wake,
Divine Presence,
signed by a flickering candle flame,
constantly available,
timelessly waiting,

wordlessly calling, inviting, embracing.
As comforting as only God can be,
in sacramental grace,
healing spirit and deep love.
"I am with you always,"
lifts and soothes and balms
our aching, longing, broken hearts.
The yoke is easy...

One thing only is better;
to be "Tabernacle" oneself,
Communioned, soul-filled,
humbly meek, unburdened,
emptied - and filled,
grace-refreshed, serenely
one with him, the Christ, Our God,
IN PEACE!

"Indeed God has made my courage fail;
the Almighty has put me in dismay.
Yes, would that I had vanished in darkness,
and that thick gloom were before me to conceal me."
Job 23:16-17

Sleepless Job

Haunting images keep drifting
in and out of sleepless dreams.
From whence comes these nightly travelers?
taunting, startling, sudden beams
which shake one's depth to wide awakening.
Slumber shifts and fades away
until the grey of dawn approaches
bringing in another day.

Are these strange nocturnal visits
messengers from some far place?

But why the crafty sly deception?
Why not meet me face to face?
Darkness cloaks the scary movements
of the mind's determined task,
as it seeks for truth and answers
and a peaceful rest at last.

"There was a man going down from Jerusalem to Jericho who fell prey to robbers. They stripped him, beat him, and then went off leaving him half-dead. A priest happened to be going down the same road; he saw him but continued on. Likewise there was a Levite who came the same way; he saw him and went on. But a Samaritan who was journeying along came on him and was moved to pity at the sight. He approached him and dressed his wounds, pouring in oil and wine...Which of these three, in your opinion, was neighbor to the man who fell in with the robbers?"   Luke 10:30-36

The Good Samaritan

Road rage!
Too new a term?
Beating? Robbing?
Leaving behind for dead? All apply, but

road rage?
Perhaps.
A road too narrow?
A path too steep?
Even for the priest,
perhaps on a mission
of his own preoccupation.
Priests are like that.

The Levite, of course, the young one,
busy - judging more complicated lives.
This case, too simple -
Just road rage!
Leave him to others, less taken.

Ah, the Samaritan!
A good man - frequent traveler.
A man who knows his way.
Knows well the road
from Jerusalem to Jericho;
Treacherous! Dangerous!
Doesn't everyone know?

Who's thumping whose breastbone
with forefinger now?
Pounding home a point of righteousness..
Many private opinions...!
But Jesus says, "It's a whole question
of neighbor..."
And, "WHO IS MINE?"

"A leper approached him with a request, kneeling down as he addressed him: 'If you will to do so, you can cure me.' Moved with pity, Jesus stretched out his hand, touched him, and said: 'I do will it. Be cured.' The leprosy left him then and there, and he was cured." Mark 1: 40-42

The Leper

The tinkling of the bell proclaimed
the presence of the man.
One "unclean", as others said,
as now they all began
to scatter from along the way,
and make room for the one
in rags and filthy rotten sores
who now approached the Son

of God to beg his gentle touch.
As on his knees he spoke
to Jesus on that day of grace,
when bonds of death he broke,
and healed the leper from his pain,
and gave him hope once more,
and sent him on his way to thank
and praise God evermore.

"From that place he went off to the territory of Tyre and Sidon.... Soon a woman, whose small daughter had an unclean spirit, heard about him. She approached him and crouched at his feet. The woman who was Greek-a Syro-Phoenician by birth - began to beg him to expel the demon from her daughter. He told her: 'Let the sons of the household satisfy themselves at table first. It is not right to take the food of the children and throw it to the dogs.' 'Please, Lord,' she replied, 'even the dogs under the table eat the family's leavings.' Then he said to her, 'For such a reply, be off now! The demon has already left your daughter.' Mark 7:24-29

The Foreigner

Pride tucked away,
faith and courage burning,
she comes.
A mother - how could she not?
Her small daughter gripped by a demon.

"It isn't right," he said abruptly.
And, momentarily, she paused,
rebuffed, not crushed.
Reflective.

Then pushed by grace,
from some far place yet unknown,
"But even the dogs
eat the family's leavings!"

What could he say
to such maternal persistence?
A mother's words at Cana,
"Do what he tells you,"
returned.

A foreigner? Yes. A Gentile? Yes.
Yet did he not come to save all?
Prophetic moment.
Compassion, healing, release.
The demon gone.
The triumph of motherhood.
There is peace!

"Whoever remains in me and I in him will bear much fruit, because without me you can do nothing...If you remain in me and my words remain in you, ask for whatever you want and it will be done for you. By this is my Father glorified, that you bear much fruit and become my disciples."   John 15: 5-8.

Starting Over

Each springtime everyone can see
the tiny blossoms on the tree,
where God will come
with gentle sun
to help it be what it should be.

Then soon, with soft and pleasant rain,
the blossoms fall and then again
will grow a shoot
to bear much fruit.

I've never heard the tree complain.
And nor do we when growth must come.
When blossoms fall when spring is done,
and in our lives
new springtime thrives
and once again, we've just begun?

"Do not fear those who deprive the body of life but cannot destroy the soul. Rather, fear him who can destroy both body and soul in Gehenna. Are not two sparrows sold for next to nothing? Yet not a single sparrow falls to the ground without your Father's consent." Matthew 10: 28-29

The Sparrows

In flurries of threes and fours or more
they suddenly come to the old back door

where a place of feeding is discovered there
and like nervous children they wonder from
    where

such an abundance comes, as they flutter and
    feast
and then fly quickly to the west and the east.

Timid souls with a wary eye
they suspect such a feast to be passing by

and perhaps tomorrow it will all be gone
and then, once more, "we will be alone."

And yet a good and kindly Father
counts each one whenever they gather,

for not one shall fall without his knowing,
and somehow it seems, in their coming and
    going

that they understand, in their own small way,
the beauty they bring to each new day.

"Meanwhile, Moses was tending the flock of his father-in-law Jethro, the priest of Midian. Leading the flock across the desert, he came to Horeb, the mountain of God. There an angel of the LORD appeared to him in fire flaming out of a bush. As he looked on, he was surprised to see that the bush, though on fire, was not consumed. So Moses decided, "I must go over to look at this remarkable sight, and see why the bush is not burned.'" Exodus 3:1-3

What Do I See?

"The leaves are on fire on the cottonwood
     tree,"
the little girl shouted as she made me see
by pulling my arm and pointing her finger
at a large old form where the sun would linger

in sudden small points of exciting light
as the angry wind's wrath, as strong as night,
was whipping and thrashing the age old tree
while pushing and nudging the little girl
  and me.

And sure enough, on the satiny finish
the fire would dance, dart, and then diminish
as it skipped and played in the fury of the
  wind
as the proud old tree would bow and bend.

Is that what Moses saw that day
so long ago in the desert way,
when God appeared and spoke to him
as the fiery bush burned and then grew dim?

I only know what I saw today--
the force of nature as God's own way,
through wind and fire unbeguiled,
of speaking to me and a little child.

"For see, the winter is past,
the rains are over and gone.
The flowers appear on the earth,
the time of pruning the vines has come,
and the song of the dove is heard in our land."
        Song of Songs 2:11-12

Spring

The reincarnation of nature.
The promise of life anew.
Proclaimed by new choirs of voices
        and colors of every hue.

"So I was left alone, seeing this great vision. No strength remained in me; I turned the color of death and was powerless. When I heard the sound of his voice, I fell face forward in a faint." Daniel 10:8-9

Alone With God

The night is still...

The breath of God
is felt upon the heart -
cautiously.

It fills the air
resounding in the soul -
silently.

The soul breathes
and with each breath it grows -
gigantically.
The sweetness of the Deity is everywhere.

Spirits move upon the senses
and prayer rises quickly to the lips.
As matter disappears at last
and hearts are wedded to their King -
in ecstasy.

The spirit swoons
in celestial contemplation -
perpetually.

And Love finds consummation
in sacramental union -
sublimely.

There is peace!

" Teacher,' they said to him, 'this woman has been caught in the act of adultery. In the law, Moses ordered such women to be stoned. What do you have to say about the case?' (They were posing this question to trap him, so that they could have something to accuse him of.) Jesus bent down and started tracing on the ground with his finger. When they persisted in their questioning, he straightened up and said to them, Let the man among you who has no sin be the first to cast a stone at her.'" John 8:4-7

Consummatum

Words in dust were boldly written.
Forgiveness for one of womanhood.
Drops of blood now write salvation
in dust beneath a cross of wood.

"Like the sparrow in its flitting, like the swallow in its flight,
a curse, uncalled-for, arrives nowhere."
   Proverbs 26:2

Swallows

Like missionaries,
zeal-filled, driven,
they sweep across
our flawed world.

Back and forth,
swiftly they come
in fervent numbers,
to purge the air
of every tiny winged thing
non-swallow.

Inquisition-like
they destroy the enemy,
deciding who should live or die;
filling their bird bellies,
growing fat,
feeding their children,
with victims.

Survival?
Balance of nature?
The graceful swallows
have their place?
And God is pleased
and so should we!

"Sing praise to the LORD, you his faithful ones,
 and give thanks to his holy name.
For his anger lasts but a moment;
a lifetime, his good will.
At nightfall, weeping enters in,
but with the dawn, rejoicing." Psalm 30:5-6

Sursuum Corda

The lazy sky is full of blue
and white,
clouds bright.
For any other foreign hue
would frighten,
fear heighten,
concern for what clouds might do.

My quiet heart is full of God;
just now
I'll bow.

Yet many other times I've trod
alone,
forlorn.
Down empty roads of guilt I'd plod.

And so the beauty of our world
was lost.
The cost?
The poverty of missing gifts all pearled,
and precious stones,
then being alone,
blind, then sight-filled to greater dreams
unfurled.

"Every man shall sit under his own vine
or under his own fig tree, undisturbed;
for the mouth of the Lord of hosts has spoken."
   Micah 4:4

Silence!

There is in every person's heart
a secret place to go.
A special sanctuary apart,
a place we seldom know.
A place where no one else may be
unless we ask them in,
so private that no one may see
how often we begin.

For only God may enter there.
It is the very place
where he alone seeks to draw near,
to bring his love and grace.

And there he whispers words of praise,
and gathers up our sins.
He turns our moments and our days
and helps us start again.

We look for him with longing eyes
and yet afraid to see.
We miss so many silent times
with him, how can that be?
Go to your secret chamber now
and welcome him with love.
For he is waiting for your call
so patiently above.

"I know a man in Christ who, fourteen years ago, whether he was in or outside his body I cannot say, only God can say - a man who was snatched up to the third heaven. I know that this man - whether in or outside his body I do not know, God knows - was snatched up to Paradise to hear words which cannot be uttered, words which no man may speak." 2 Corinthians 12:2-4

Ecstasy

Stepping into contemplation,
closing doors of spoken word.
Settling into concentration,
turning to the Risen Lord.

Seeking silence in the quiet,
focusing on Jesus there.
Finding space so deep and private
from anxiety and care.

O the heart in beauty's splendor
opens wide its welcome door;
waiting in majestic grandeur,
never as it's been before.

Coming now in grace and blessing,
humble servant, King of Kings,
bringing rich and rubied dressing,
lifting hearts on sacred wings.

Quickly now do we consider
what a gift to be conceived;
not in vain and foolish glitter
but in mysteries now believed.

Resting now in Spirit's comfort,
so serenely do we pray.
Wordless as the souls in God's court,
peacefully, we long to stay.

"Bless the LORD, O my soul!
O lord, my God you are great indeed!
You are clothed with majesty and glory,
 robed in light as with a cloak...
You make the clouds your chariot;
you travel on the wings of the wind...
Beside them the birds of heaven dwell;
from among the branches they send forth their song."
Psalm 104:1-3, 12

Wild Petunias

The pale purple blossoms,
like dreams untouched,
dance in the gentle summer breeze.
Ballet-like they swirl and dip,
softly keeping time
to the music of the day,

hummed by tiny feathered be-winged
creatures of God,
frenzied in their movements,
keeping the curious swallows guessing
in their swooping search.

The gossip of the sparrows
marks the tempo,
as clouds roll by in quiet majesty
and buzzing bees with sticky feet
spread pollen
and an attitude of busyness,
shaming the lazy sunshine
as it gently warms the world
with a need for noontime rest
in its drowsiness.
It is June!

"Why is my pain continuous,
my wound incurable, refusing to be healed?
You have indeed become for me a treacherous brook,
whose waters do not abide! Thus, the LORD
answered me: If you repent, so that I restore you,
in my presence you shall stand...
And I will make you toward this people
a solid wall of brass.'" Jeremiah 15:18-20

Recovery

Like teasing and dancing butterfly wings,
brushing and breathing on sensitive things,
is the muted feeling of invisible touch,
soft, then firm, then not that much.

The pain, once sharp, is fading away
and the numbing presence begins to sway.
The tidal waves which ebb and flow
from shore to shore now come and go.

The tickle and taunt of sight and sound
seem to rise and wrap themselves round,
as the finger of God and its healing touch
soothes and strengthens and comforts so
    much.

But then an explosion of sorts is there,
whipping tranquility into the air,
as pin-points of pain again rise and fall,
and suddenly seem not there at all.

And so, thus the process of healing takes
    place--
moments of suffering and moments of grace,
quietly bringing new strength and scope
to God's patient people, still suffering in hope.

"Come by yourselves to an out-of-the-way place and rest a little." Mark 6:31

My Summer Place

The time has come for my return,
as now my heart begins to yearn
for that small place beside the sea
which God himself prepared for me.

That place of quiet, place of rest,
where swallows come to build their nests;
and robins seem to think that they
have ownership, as well they may.

For they come first, in early spring
with nests to build and songs to sing,
to welcome blossoms on the boughs
and train their young, as time allows.

The gentle lake is calling me.
The calm and quiet of the sea
like soothing music calls me home,
now that winter is over and gone.

I must go back to my Summer Place,
where I will live my summer pace.
Where with my friends, the birds and bees,
I'll revel in the gentle breeze.

Where God and I will share our lives;
where peace serenely comes and thrives,
and then when all my years are past,
my Summer Place will be my last.

And I will set my soul at rest,
for having known and loved the best
of life here in this place of grace,
at last I'll see him face to face.

"As the new heavens and the new earth
which I will make
shall endure before me, says the LORD,
so shall your race and your name endure.
From one new moon to another,
and from one sabbath to another,
all mankind shall come to worship before me, says the
LORD." Isaiah 66:22-23

Moonlight on Lake Tschida

The silver satin ripples
on the moon lit lake
beckon me to follow,
inviting me to take
a voyage into beauty,
adventure and escape.

Down the glimmering highway
into depths of mystery,

my spirit flees the confines
of human history
and sparkles in the moonlight
upon the candled sea.

"I called upon your name, O LORD,
from the bottom of the pit;
 you heard me call, Let not your ear be deaf to my
cry for help!'
You came to my aid when I called to you;
you said, Have no fear!' " Lamentations 3:55-57

The White Rose

It stands so tall and sentry-like
on the bedside table,
lifting its pale white petals
to its Creator in silent prayer.

The hospital sleeps; a deep yet restless
    slumber,
like a gentle, caring mother
exhausted from the daily concerns and needs
of her children, as they come and go.

The "patient" - sleepless - feels the pulse
of pain and healing -
the ebb and flow of life,
strong and weak,
blood and water,
bone and flesh,
struggling to be stronger -
all around him.

He studies the rose
and is uplifted.
He remembers the pain and
the surgeon's effort to remove
the relentless malignant invader
from his body,
and to spare and preserve
the healthy tissue.
And now it is over - and he rests!

And, yes, now in the dark of night,
struck by the beauty of that single white
    rose,
he is moved to find words

of praise and thanksgiving,
and to lift them up on deep feelings
of gratitude - inspired by that
one white rose
which speaks so eloquently
OF HEALING!

"A great sign appeared in the sky, a woman clothed with the sun, with the moon under her feet, and on her head a crown of twelve stars." Revelations 12:1

Tepeyac Hill

The pathways wind round Tepeyac
where children run and play.
But Juan Diego, on that morn,
was on his way to pray.

She seemed alone and somewhat shy
when she caught his eye that day.
And since his hurried mission called,
he hoped she'd go away.

Another path would solve his need.
But, wait, she's come there too.
"Sweet Mother, must you bother me?
My uncle's ill, it's true."

"Please listen now to me, my son.
My message you must carry
to those who have authority,
now go and do not tarry."

"A chapel in this rugged place?
The bishop must be told?
The roses will convince him now?
So many, my arms hold."

And then, behold, her picture there.
The Virgin Mother's present
to show her love and gentle care
through this humble, faithful peasant.

Now to the world is told the story
of Juan Diego's grace,
of Our Lady's image and its glory
on Tepeyac's Holy Place.

"Up Jerusalem! stand upon the heights;
look to the east and see your children
Gathered from the east and west
at the word of the Holy One,
rejoicing that they are remembered by God."
  Baruch 5:5

Desert City

O history laden place
where ancient myths abound.
Where missionaries touched your soul
and faith sprung from your depths.

A sacred, mystical way of life,
profoundly holy - desert touched.
So young at heart, yet so primitive.
So new and exciting, yet so old and wise.

Small town grown up,
stretching your generous arms
to embrace all colors and creeds
clutching them to your mountainous bosom.

O Desert City, so proud, so patient,
cactus-filled - threatening -
and yet, warm, loving and soothing,
healing and comforting the unwell -
   Christ-like!

Violence can hardly touch
the casual calmness of your being.
Your blue sky days and glittering starry nights
belie the vigorous energy of your soul.

The daily hustle and bustle keeps time
to the steady flow of life in the beating of
   your heart,
pulsing in the summer's heat!
Tucson, we love you!

"But if you do not heed me and do not keep all these commandments, if you reject my precepts and spurn my decrees, refusing to obey all my commandments and breaking my covenant, then I, in turn, will give you your deserts. I will punish you with terrible woes - with wasting and fever to dim the eyes and sap the life...I will turn against you, till you are beaten down before your enemies and lorded over by your foes. You will take to flight though no one pursues you."
Leviticus 26:14-17

Cactus Land

Devastation!
The elegant cactus plant
so proud and silent,
in a beauty singular,
lies in ragged pieces.

Like fallen leaves,
its thorny cover
and spiny spears
are no match for the sharp-edged tool
in the hands of his destroyer.

It seemed so secure,
so fortress-like,
protected,
embattled,
so strong and fierce against all odds,
except the determined human force,
overpowering,
conquering and subduing,
destroying its life.

Its sin?
It had grown too quickly.
Too proudly.
As threatening as war.
Encroaching upon space not its own,

space where other,
more lovely plants
might live and grow
and pleasure us.

So it is gone!
And it teaches us a lesson
in its going.
Too big...too soon,
too proud...overpowering
sometimes are we!

Then comes the sharpness
of word or action
to prune and shape,
and oftentimes uproot,
so that a new and better life
may ultimately grow,
bear abundant fruit,
and bring us joy!

"Whoever welcomes a child such as this for my sake welcomes me. And whoever welcomes me welcomes, not me, but him who sent me." Mark 9:37.

Eight Years Old

He would often come to visit me
on an afternoon of school.
He would sit and chat the time away,
with his pencils, books and rule.

I often thought, while "adult-like,"
he spun philosophy,
"oft time from out the mouths of babes"
has found identity.

His great desires were all made known
in the confidence he found
while talking "man to man" with me,
and kicking topics round.

His dreams were often fairytaled
by things he'd seen or heard
from older boys from "fourth" and up,
for he was just in "third."

His hopes and fears, I learned, were real,
in secrets that we shared.
Companionship is what he sought -
and proudly knew I cared.

On rainy days his feet were wet
for his galoshes he'd forgot.
And his mother's scold, he would lament
as homeward he would trot.

His eyes would shine with real love
while making his goodbyes,
and promises of "another time"
from smiling lips would rise.

I haven't seen him now for years
and maybe won't again.
But I have often prayed to God
that the simple path of life he trod
while passing by each "Homer's nod"
would beckon other men!

"From the rising to the setting of the sun
is the name of the LORD to be praised.
High above all nations is the lord,
above the heavens is his glory."
   Psalm 113: 3-4

A New Day

Some mornings when I cannot sleep
I like to watch the sunshine creep
into my world as darkness fades
and dew appears upon the blades
of grass, which formed the night before,
as shadows fall across the floor
and life again, like sudden birth,
springs into being upon the earth.

Another gift from God on high
is each new day as time goes by,
and we, like children, lost in play,
accept his gifts in casual ways

and take each day as though we've earned
it, never sure of what we've learned
about our place in God's own plan
or what he really thinks of man.

And so we watch the daylight come
to lure us into life begun
again, with prayers to say and things to do.
It's almost as if life is new
and simply will forever last,
although so many days have passed
and God alone knows which are left
as in and out of dreams we drift.

But until time itself runs out,
I'll greet the days and sing and shout
with grateful heart for all God gives,
and with each soul, who daily lives
and knows that God is one who cares,
I'll thank him for my world which shares
its sunshine and its rain, it seems,
to give me time to share my dreams.

"The voice of the LORD is over the waters,
the God of glory thunders,
the LORD, over vast waters.
The voice of the LORD is mighty;
the voice of the LORD is majestic."
　　Psalm 29:3-4

Cannon Beach

The gentle, soothing sound of surf
is rhythmic to my ears,
as ocean waves come tumbling in
to wash away my fears.

The mournful moaning of the sea,
like some far distant sound,
invites my cradled heart to rest
in quiet slumber found.

The foam along the water's edge
has trimmed the shore with lace,
as gentle breezes come and go,
yet leaving not a trace

of movement on the tranquil beach
where footsteps slowly pass;
and prints of former feet are gone
like leaves among the grass.

From out the rolling, rumbling tides,
is that God's voice we hear?
Majestically it calls to us
to tell us he is near.

O time, you softly move along
and life is lived each day,
as timeless motion drives the swell
and holds the world in sway.

The beauty of the surging waves,
the pensive mood they bring,
serenely cloaks my restless heart
and lifts my soul to sing.

"I had thought:
How I should like to treat you as sons,
And give you a pleasant land,
a heritage most beautiful among the nations!
You would call me, my Father,' I thought,
and never cease following me.
But like a woman faithless to her lover,
even so have you been faithless to me,
O House of Israel, says the LORD."

    Jeremiah 3:19-

Where is God?

In the silence of my heart
I seek someone.
In the clutter of my life
I am alone.
In the darkness of my days
I find no one.
The one whom I long for
is gone.

My nights are all dream-filled
and restless
with moments of wonder
and fear.
In the long shadowed movements
of searching,
I desperately pray
you are near.

I reach for your love
in the morning.
In prayer I believe
it can be
that a new revelation
is coming
and a new joy is dawning
in me!

"During the meal he took bread, blessed and broke it, and gave it to them. Take this,' he said, this is my body.' He likewise took a cup, gave thanks and passed it to them, and they all drank from it. He said to them: This is my blood, the blood of the covenant, to be poured out on behalf of many.'" Mark 14:22-25

Memories

Little girls in dresses white,
and boys in navy blue,
make their way with candles bright,
we wonder how they grew.

The freshness of their faith and love,
the beauty of their smile,
amazes us, like summer doves
who come and rest awhile.

We once were innocent and young.
We, too, were full of hope.
How is it that our dreams have sprung
and left us here to grope?

We cannot now retrace our steps;
each one, the path must trod.
For in our journey through the depths,
we seek and find our God.

In Eucharistic memories
our souls are young again,
the life we live is not our own
for Christ has entered in.

"Happy the man who meditates on wisdom,
and reflects on knowledge;
Who ponders her ways in his heart, and understands
her paths..." Sirach 14:20-21

Holy Wisdom

How often would I change my course
had I the power to go?
Would then I new directions take
and have the grace to know
where weakness lies in daily strife,
where strength can be applied,
where virtue comes more easily,
where sin can be denied?

But life is lived sometimes by chance
and days are moments tolled;
like moving through the hours, so brief,
as sometimes uncontrolled.

We walk our path with feeble steps;
we falter as we go.
Yet tortured hearts in symphonies
still pleasing shadows show.
Around the cross of pain and tears
the fragile blossoms grow,
to promise yet more gentle years
of music in my soul.

Saint Patrick was born in Great Britain about the year 385. As a young man, he was captured and sold as a slave in Ireland where he had to tend sheep. Having escaped from slavery, he chose to enter the priesthood, and later, as a bishop, he returned to Ireland and tirelessly preached the Gospel to the people of Ireland where he converted many to the faith and established the church. He died at Down, Ireland, in 461. (*Liturgy of the Hours,* March 17)

O Shepherd Boy

Dear Patrick, poor lone shepherd boy,
lost in ancient story.
Individually called by God
to a life of Irish glory.

Called to bring a distant faith
to a land of mystery.
Chosen to proclaim this gift
through the days of history.

O Shepherd Boy, how could you know
the great plans God had for you?
As priested son you then returned
and preached old faith made new.

The gentle touch of word and song,
the simple, "Shamrock Story"
converted pagan knights and kings
and gave Ireland its glory.

O Shepherd Man, O Bishop, called
to gather lambs and sheep,
now take your rest among your flock,
and with them, may you sleep.

"The LORD said to Abram: Look about you, and from where you are, gaze to the north and south, east and west; all the land that you see I will give to you and your descendants forever.'"   Genesis 13:14-15

Kyleva

Kyleva, O Kyleva,
from whence my family sprung,
where candles burn on Holy Days
and chapel bells are rung.

Kyleva, O Kyleva,
so small a place to see;
in Hugginstown the graveyard holds
what my family used to be.

Where wars were fought and lives were lost
for truth and liberty.
Where families lived and loved their faith
in strength and dignity.

O Kyleva, so rich and grand,
so filled with memories.
And yet, so poor in many ways,
except in destinies.

A special spot in Kilkenny land,
so rimmed with mountains 'round,
the beauty of your countryside
alone, held no one bound.

And so it was that Grandpa John
felt free to leave this place;
to seek his fortune and his faith
in prayer, and with God's grace.

O Kyleva, do you recall
that fateful day he sailed?
In spite of parents' anxious pleas,
his searching heart prevailed.

So, Kyleva, I must go back
to pay my great respects
to generations of my folks
as Kyleva expects.

To see my friends, like family,
"Millea" is their name,
who welcome me at Kyleva
and make it quite the same
as when the ancient kinsmen lived
and loved this place so much,
I bend my knee and bow my head
in reverence for such
a chance to lift my thoughts
in thankful prayer and song,
in Kyleva, my ancient home,
where, now, my heart belongs.

"Every high priest is taken from among men and made their representative before God, to offer gifts and sacrifices for sins. He is able to deal patiently with erring sinners, for he himself is beset by weakness and so must make sin offerings for himself as well as for the people. One does not take this honor on his own initiative, but only when called by God as Aaron was." Hebrews 5:1-4

Priest Forever

Hands which once were only man
are strangely God-like now;
as lifted they absolve and bless
or sooth a troubled brow.

Lips now formed in Sacred Words
pronounce, and lo! Behold,

where once was wine, his blood now flows,
and bread, his limbs enfold.

For God has chosen other selves
new journeys to begin;
and where there once was only man,
now Christ has entered in.

"Come to me, all you who labor and are burdened, and I will give you rest. Take my yoke upon you and learn from me, for I am meek and humble of heart; and you will find rest for yourselves. For my yoke is easy, and my burden light." Matthew 11:28-30

Grex Meus

Tainted souls around him clamored,
their sins to have relieved.
Then sainted souls, each grace enamored,
with love and faith believed.

"O LORD, hear my prayer,
and let my cry come to you.
Hide not your face from me
in the day of my distress.
Incline your ear to me;
in the day when I call, answer me speedily."
  Psalm 102:1-3

Matins

"Deus in adjutorium meum intende,"
the monks begin to pray.
"Domine ad adjuvandum me festina,"
with fervent hope they say.

They greet the sun with joyful chant
as morning breaks again.
They lift their rested voices now
as together they begin

a new day filled with work and prayer,
like ancient monks of old,
they dedicate their lives to God,
as praying hands they fold.

Persistent lips profess their love
in verses strong and clear,
as heaven-ward, like incense raised,
go thoughts that God is near.

Then bowing low they recognize
the Trinity of Three;
God, Father, Son and Spirit blest
they serve on bended knee.

As all the sleeping countryside
continues its own pace,
the monks, in prayer, lift up all things,
and touch the world with grace.

"Man goes forth to his work
and to his tillage till the evening.
How manifold are your works, O LORD!
In wisdom you have wrought them all -
the earth is full of your creatures."
    Psalm 104:23-24

Twilight

Softly comes the evening now
like unexpected guests,
darkening the world below
as silently it rests

upon the quiet countryside
where, quickening its pace,
the light of day seems to confide
its farewell to embrace.

Blanket-wise it comforts us
in muted sounds so blest.
As grateful for God's daily trust,
we give ourselves to rest.

"The voice of the LORD is mighty;
the voice of the LORD is majestic.
The voice of the LORD breaks the cedars,
the LORD breaks the cedars of Lebanon...
the voice of the LORD shakes the desert,
the LORD shakes the wilderness of Kadesh..."
    Psalm 29:4-8

Angry is the Night

The angry night berates the world
in sharp and thunderous tones,.
a "temper tantrum," so it seems
while all of nature groans.

Why, O night, are you so troubled?
Why carry on this way?
Most other times you seem serene,
and peaceful, like the day.

But now you push your weight around,
you trample trees and fields,
you rush around in wild pursuit
as all creation shields

itself from outbursts you impose
on everything around,
until, at last, you settle down
and quiet calm is found.

Why must you cause so much concern
by seeming out of hand?
Don't you know that we prefer
contentment in our land?

So let your quiet starry sky
shine brightly once again,
to guide the weary, lead the strong,
and lift the world from pain.

"Full authority has been given to me both
in heaven and on earth;
go, therefore, and make disciples of all the nations...
Teach them to carry out everything I have
commanded you.
And know that I am with you always, until
the end of the world!"

Matthew 28:18-20

Presence

Silently it creeps upon me
as I gaze upon the light.
Sudden, certain, strange awareness
of his presence, strength and might.

Like the dawning of the daylight
softly touches shapes and sounds.
So the beauty of his presence
fills the world where he abounds.

Touching hearts and healing wounded
souls, with just a measured gift of grace.
Turning them to look and search for
his compassionate, loving face.

"Ever since we heard this we have been praying for you unceasingly and asking that you may attain full knowledge of his will through perfect wisdom and spiritual insight. Then you will lead a life worthy of the Lord and pleasing to him in every way. You will multiply good works of every sort and grow in the knowledge of God." Col. 1:9-10

Saint Fiacre, Hermit

O holy, humble hermit,
saint of your time,
called and chosen,
caught up in the rush to ancient abbeys,
seeking salvation...listen!

Solitude!
You loved and devoutly sought it
in quiet hermitage
in Ireland and then in France,
tilling your garden's soil,
while tilling the garden of your soul.

Swept up in singular beauty,
seeking always Beauty Himself,
in growing things,
in nature's gifts,
in graced moments of contemplation.

O, holy, humble hermit, St. Fiacre,
patron of gardeners;
help us to grow in our own sacred space,
silently, devoutly, like yourself,
in praise of our Creator!

"The heavens proclaim your wonders, O LORD,
and your faithfulness, in the assembly of the holy
ones.
For who in the skies rank with the lord?
Who is like the lord among the sons of God?"
    Psalm 89:6-7

Sunset

A splash of grandeur across the sky;
the glory of God is displayed.
Orange-reds and colors unknown before,
in a moment all life is delayed.

And suddenly, the world stands still,
the birds are quiet and hushed,
as a glimpse of Tabor, in brilliant hues,
across the sky is brushed.

The vision of God, as he dwells in heaven,
is hardly more glorious than this,
but as we wait to share it some day,
this gift of the future is his.

The quiet of night begins to descend,
the day's goodness and evil are done.
And darkness embraces our world again
and sleep and rest have begun.

"Yours are the heavens, and yours is the earth;
the world and its fullness you have founded."
Psalm 89:12

Music for the Heart

"Jesus,"
a song in the heart,
unsung, waiting
until that moment,
when touched by grace,
the stone is rolled back,
and the music starts,
and the song is sung,
and the spirit is free.

"Jesus,"
sweet melody to the lips,
the Song of Songs,
rising, lifting and embracing;
the music of the heart!
Fresh and new, LIKE SPRING!

"It was now about noon and darkness came over the whole land until three in the afternoon because of an eclipse of the sun." Luke 23:44

Eclipse

Softly the shadow creeps forward.
Like the curtain of night it falls
across the face of the shining moon
and darkness descends like a pall.

Soon shapes and sounds are muted
and an eery feeling comes down
on every child and creature of God
like a sudden rebuke or frown.

Changing the heart and its beating,
from joy to wonder and pain.
Until the shadow again passes through,
and the whole world smiles again.

"Oh, that I were as in the months past!
as in the days when God watched over me,
While he kept his lamp shining above my head,
and by his light I walked through darkness;
as I was in my flourishing days,
when God sheltered my tent."   Job 29:1-4

Shadows

Reaching into history's pages,
seeking days of long ago,
searching memories of past ages,
lifting scenes so far below.

The consciousness of present places,
yearning for the years gone by,
stored away in dusty spaces
far beyond the gazing eye.

Curious images of living,
skeptical of sudden thought,
coming clear in time for giving
meaning to the days we've brought.

Haunting dreams of former failings,
casting shadows on my heart;
causing me to wish for healing,
fleeing memories fall apart.

Wondering about life's ending,
coming back to present times,
future dreams will now be pending,
as we live our lives in rhymes.

"O LORD, to you I call; hasten to me;
hearken to my voice when I call upon you.
Let my prayer come like incense before you;
the lifting up of my hands, like the evening sacrifice."
  Psalm 141:1-2

Vesper Song

Bending knees in adoration,
folding hands in quiet prayer,
closing eyes in contemplation,
finding God is present there.

Thinking loving thoughts of beauty,
moving lips in gentle tones,
bowing heads in prayerful poses,
knowing we are not alone.

In the quiet time of evening,
as the vesper bell does ring,
from our hearts in true devotion,
praise of God, we start to sing.

All creation soon is hushed
and the dark of night descends,
as the music of our singing
fervently to God ascends.

At the ending of the daylight,
prayers of thankfulness and praise
lift our hearts and heal our spirits,
as we live our grateful days.

"And now, brothers, I must say good-bye. Mend your ways. Encourage one another. Live in harmony and peace, and the God of love and peace will be with you. Greet one another with a holy kiss. All the holy ones send greetings to you." 2 Corinthians 13:11-12

Gone Away

Questions come and questions go
and in their midst I stay.
What will they say when I am gone,
when I have gone away?

"And does it matter much at all?"
I ask myself each day.
And in my heart I know it does,
when I have gone away.

Will they remember what I did,
or what I said or say?
Will some few words remain behind,
when I have gone away?

The memories of our lives, we build
as we live life day by day.
What memories will I leave behind
when I have gone away?

Will my friends weep and miss the kind
of things I'd do and say?
Or will they soon forget it all
when I have gone away?

So, does it really matter much,
as I kneel here and pray;
what others cling to of my life
when I have gone away?

For after all it's really true,
unless I go astray,
it's God alone whose love endures
when I have gone away

So to my family and my friends,
I say farewell today.
My love and prayers will be with you
when I have gone away.

Do not grieve and long for me,
my heart at last is free.
For God, who loves me most of all,
now hugs me constantly.

Amen.

"Do not conform yourselves to this age but be transformed by the renewal of your mind, so that you may judge what is God's will, what is good, pleasing and perfect."   Romans 12:2

Conformity

Conformity has never been
a passion of my soul;
to be like everybody else
so often takes its toll.

To dress and live as current fads
dictate for everyone,
it seems to me should never be
the choice of one begun

To search for other ways
of self-expression forms,
by being just as God intends,
not caught in human norms.

And yet, my need to be conformed
to him who sets the pace,
is strong and passionate as well,
and calls me to his grace.

How often I am torn between
the "now" and the "yet to be."
How fervently I pray each day
for wisdom so I see

the difference in the worlds which seek
to capture my poor heart.
Sometimes I live the "now" I know;
sometimes I live "apart."

Since heaven waits, I must prepare
my soul, this is the key.
So, I'll conform, not to the "now,"
but to the "yet to be."

"I am the vine, you are the branches.
He who lives in me and I in him,
will produce abundantly,
for apart from me you can do nothing."
    John 15:5

Life's Autumn

The green leaves now are turning brown,
as yellows and reds abound.
A touch of fall is in the air
and frost is on the ground.
Another summer soon is gone.
The months pass quickly by.
The summer sun is fading fast
as geese south bound now fly.

The season's flowers have lost their bloom.
Cucumber vines are drying.
The chill of winter is everywhere,
and summer's beauty is dying.

How quickly come and quickly go
the seasons of each year.
Like life, which seems to pass so soon,
proclaims the end is near.

And God, Creator of it all,
just gathers in his arms
the beauty of each person's soul
to save it from what harms.
Just like the flowers of the field
which wither and are gone,
so God calls each of us back home
when growing time is done.

How much like nature's mysteries
are we, God's special gift;
as life on earth, its ebb and flow,
seeks energy to lift
itself from here below
back to its sacred source,
to God, who welcomes us with love
when life has run its course.

"See what love the Father has bestowed on us that we may be called children of God. Yet so we are. The reason the world does not know us is that it did not know him. Beloved, we are God's children now; what we shall be has not yet been revealed. We do know that when it is revealed we shall be like him, for we shall see him as he is." First Letter of John 3:1-2

Heaven Waits

What is it like to be with God?
The question gently starts to prod
my heart to search for other things
which suddenly and slowly brings
my thoughts to think of heaven's place
awaiting me and all who grace
this humble world in which we live
and where we do our best to give

to all some sense of where we'll go
when life is over here below.

Is God just waiting patiently
for us to come so he can see
how glad we are to be with him?
I wonder, as we cut and trim
our prayers each morning of each day,
does he just wait and never say
a word to question our good deeds
as in our hands, our rosary beads
are counted out at random pace,
and don't we often seem to race
right through our moments set aside
for God, or is it just our pride?

I often wonder how it is
to be in heaven, which is his
own promise for us all.
It is not easy to recall.
Do angels sing or fly around
on clouds so soft and are they crowned
like saints who smile and never frown,

and all is quiet up and down
the corridors of heaven's court?
I've heard it said in one report.

Or is it much more like our earth,
where laughter, song and even mirth
will often fill the air with sound
like children laughing all around?
And are there ice cream cones and sweets
and jelly beans and special treats
to keep us happy all day long,
and do the angels lead the song
when we all sing with voices sweet
with no "off key," which is a treat?
So can one somersault and flip
if suddenly we hop and skip
as children often used to do
when I was young, and pretty new?

What is it like to be with God?
I think I need again to prod
my heart to think a little more
about what heaven has in store

for me when all is said and done
and my new life will have begun.
It sounds exciting and I guess
it will be just the very best

of everything our God can give
to each of us so we can live
with him in joy and perfect peace
when from this earth we have release.

Exciting as it really is
I guess I'm not much of a whiz
for queuing up for heaven's gate,
I only hope I won't be late
when Peter calls me home at last,
I'm sure I'll hurry very fast
to see my God for whom I live,
and all I have I then will give
to him forever with my heart.
The best is that we'll never part!

So do not say I cannot go
when life is over here below!

My soul aches for that new place
to see my Savior face to face
and never have to leave his side
but with him always to abide
in love, and never feeling pain
or lonely times ever again.

And so I set my anxious heart
on heaven's joy, which seems to start
my longing for that place of rest
where none of us is just a guest
but rather we will be at home
where we belong. No more alone.
Instead, with family and friends
we'll live that life which never ends;
where God, our loving Father waits
to welcome us through heaven's gates.
Where peace and joy will come to be
our gifts to share ETERNALLY.

Amen.